TRUST

CLEVELAND STATE UNIVERSITY POETRY CENTER
PRIZE WINNING TITLES

2008   Liz Waldner, *Trust*
       Allison Benis White, *Self-Portrait with Crayon*
2007   Linda Lee Harper, *Kiss, Kiss*
       Bern Mulvey, *The Fat Sheep Everyone Wants*
2006   Barbara Presnell, *Piece Work*
       Sam Witt, *Sunflower Brother*
2005   Christopher Burawa, *The Small Mystery of Lapses*
       Max Garland, *Hunger Wide as Heaven*
2003   Doug Goetsch, *The Job of Being Everybody*
       Mary Quade, *Guide to Native Beasts*
2002   Sarah Kennedy, *Double Exposure*
       Eliot Khalil Wilson, *The Saint of Letting Small Fish Go*
2001   Deirdre O'Connor, *Before the Blue Hour*
2000   Alison Luterman, *The Largest Possible Life*
1999   Carol Potter, *Short History of Pets*
1998   Dan Bellm, *Buried Treasure*
1997   Judith Vollmer, *The Door Open to the Fire*
1996   Marilyn Krysl, *Warscape with Lovers*
1995   Robert Hill Long, *The Work of the Bow*
1994   Amy Newman, *Order, or Disorder*
1993   Claudia Rankine, *Nothing in Nature is Private*
1992   Susan Firer, *The Lives of the Saints and Everything*
1991   Richard Jackson, *Alive All Day*
1990   Robert Kendall, *A Wandering City*
1989   Sarah Provost, *Inland, Thinking of Waves*
1988   Stephen Tapscott, *Another Body*
1987   Trish Reeves, *Returning the Question*

LIZ WALDNER

TRUST

Winner of the 2008 Cleveland State University Poetry Center Open Competition

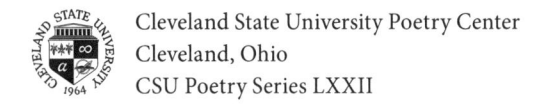

Cleveland State University Poetry Center
Cleveland, Ohio
CSU Poetry Series LXXII

Copyright © 2009 by Liz Waldner
All rights reserved

Printed in the United States of America
Printed on acid-free paper

5   4   3   2   1

First edition

This book is the winner of the 2008 Cleveland State University Poetry Center Open Competition, selected by an Editorial Committe comprised of Kazim Ali, Mary Biddinger, Michael Dumanis, and Sarah Gridley. This book is a title in the CSU Poetry Series published by the Cleveland State University Poetry Center, 2121 Euclid Avenue, Cleveland, Ohio, 44115-2214. www.csuohio.edu/poetrycenter

Book design by BookMatters, Berkeley
Set in Minion
Cover design by Amy Freels
Cover art by Julie Heffernan

Library of Congress Cataloging-in-Publication Data

Waldner, Liz.
    Trust : poems / by Liz Waldner. —1st ed.
       p.   cm. — (CSU poetry series ; 72)
    ISBN 978-1-880834-84-8 (alk. paper)
    I. Cleveland State University. Poetry Center. II. Title. III. Series.

PS3573.A42158T78   2009
811'.54—dc22   2008054543

"What sort of insects do you rejoice in, where you come from?" the gnat inquired. "I don't rejoice in insects at all," Alice explained, "because I'm rather afraid of them—at least the large kinds. But I can tell you the names of some of them."

LEWIS CARROLL

History is the process of discovering the uses of things . . .

KARL MARX

CONTENTS

i. Eye

    Truth, Beauty, Tree   / 5
    My Hand   / 6
    Novice   / 8
    Chameleon   / 9
    Crocodile Smiles   / 10
    Booking It   / 11
    Coming Through, It Got Nice   / 14
    On the Way   / 15
    Lecture   / 16
    In Some Respects Invisible, She Greets the Poet   / 24
    Trust   / 25

ii. Skin

    The Uses of Things   / 23
    Terrible Two's   / 24
    Taking the Air   / 25
    Trojan Ho(u/r)se-keeping   / 27
    There was a comely note of poignancy in his insistence at the table that making love is like in its pleasure to the eating of an Orange.   / 28
    On Losing One's Life   / 30
    Another House on Mother's Day   / 31
    Forked Song   / 32
    Necessity with Respect to Yes   / 34
    Passing   / 36
    Assumption   / 38

iii. Mouth

Yew-berry   /   41
Persephone Tells About
    Some Goings Down   /   42
Now We Are Sick(x)   /   44
Present Company Occluded   /   45
The Au Pair Girl's Speech   /   46

iv. Nose

Point, Counterpoint   /   49
Amen (On Christmas Day)   /   50
Miracle Whip or, Every Angel His
    Own B(r)e(a)dspread   /   51
Bud Cabal I   /   53
Annunciation   /   55

v. Ear

Invitation   /   59
Shame   /   60
You Can Talk to the Animas   /   61
Dream of Hat and Mouth   /   62
Apostrophe Antiphonal   /   64
Speaking (Out) of Feeling   /   66
With the Tongues of Angels   /   67
Covenant   /   69

ACKNOWLEDGMENTS

Artful Dodge	"Dream of Hat and Mouth"
	"Novice"
	"Passing"
The Denver Quarterly	'Truth, Beauty, Tree"
	"The Uses of Things"
The Iowa Review	"Amen (On Christmas Day)"
	"Bud Cabal I"
	"My Hand"
The Massachusetts Review	"With the Tongues of Angels"
New American Writing	"On the Way"
New Letters	"Trojan Ho(u/r)se-keeping"
The Northwest Review	"Assumption"
Shenandoah	"The Au Pair Girl's Speech"
13th Moon	"Booking It"
	"There was a comely note . . ."

Thanks also to the Massachusetts Cultural Council for its Individual Artist Poetry Fellowship, the City of Somerville for an Arts Grant, the Barbara Deming Money for Women Fund, and the MacDowell Colony, *sine qua non*.

TRUST

i. Eye

"*Are you a botanist, Dr. Johnson?*"

"*No sir, I am not a botanist, and should I wish to become a botanist, I must first turn myself into a reptile.*"

SAMUEL JOHNSON

Truth, Beauty, Tree

> . . . *only when he discerns beauty itself through what makes it visible will he be quickened with the true virtue.* —Plato's *Symposium*, 212a

Such embroidery of the green
    Body. The sky
Is a beautiful wound
    In it. I
Would like this not to be
    True but it is.
Nor is it useful—like the eye
    Itself the sight
We hope to see through (to)
    Always.

My Hand

My hand is like a house to me
Thin, like the rest of me
Small, hard—
It's a perfectly good hand.

When I was a child
I lived in this hand
In the thin, hard light
Of that time

In the fingernails
Drawn down like shades
So inside something
Bad can happen

In perfectly good daylight.

When I come out, I come out the door
Way my hands make for me
Making me
My own bright threshold.

Before I go out
I hold my own hand
I raise the shades
So I can see

A cat
A dog
A horse
A shelter

All perfectly good.

Novice

The baby maples hold out their hands:
"As you can see, there is nothing to see that you cannot see."

I forgive them. I only wish that I were so certain.

The ant has no back. He is three beads
Strung on an impetus that means "Everything is necessary."

He means 'for me' where "me" means "him." I believe him.

The starling whistles, then rattles the bones
Of his throat on top the antenna to the neighbor's tv.

When he flew, he left the skin of his motion.
This I could see.

Chameleon

If you appear to me a leaf the green of the laurel's
I become that leaf-green.

If I judge you bluer, like the spruce,
I agonize to match that hue.

If it seems to me the laurel approves what it's seen
I gather my energies and elaborate its green.

Such crises, researches, calculations—
The abysses attendant on such trials!

An unexpected rattle
Of dry leaf alarms me:

Dissatisfaction?
A clearing of the throat as if to leave?

Fallen short of congruency,
The crow will eat me.

Already its feathered shadow falls
Away from my claws.

Crocodile Smiles

She doesn't want it. Her smile does it.
She, the daughter, is mother then,
Smiling along with her classmates. Her arm
Topples like a pine. There's forgiveness
In the way it hits the table, she sees.
Her children don't know her; nevertheless
Her heart quickens when she catches one's eyes—
Maybe something will come of it, all these
Tree-cutters in the woods, their
Toothed saws, all these
Needles, north lost, crumbs
Eaten and the door bolted
At home.

Booking It

When I came out of the library
(gargoyles; a stone in the ground says EUCLID),
a Chinese man was sitting on a bench
cutting his toenails. It was evening,
it was going to rain. He was young.
The beech tree's new copper
and the snippets of paper that offer
a phone number for "House Cleanling"
(flyer hung on light pole) trembled.
The light changed. "Cleanling"
makes it sound so sweetly sleek
and creaturely. Changeling.

[Here, internal monologue ensues:
Mr. Jing-a-ling, how you ring-a-ling,
keeper of the keys. . . . Married to the maker
of *The Key to All Mythologies*—Miss Bronte,
how could you do it to Dorothea?]

Any old evening in Oz
and yrs truly is dismayed
(crescent moons of keratin-man
encrust the red brick walk),
wonders how somebody got to feel

that allowed in the world.
A point is that which has no part
(Euclid's definition). Analysand,
apparition, say ah. Say I (pearl
of great price, assayed, a steal)
can't even stand
and look when I want, never mind
leave a litter of me behind.

Oh, these leavings.
Elves come and turn them into shoes.
Making my way through the dark woods
I leave again and again.
Daphne in Albuquerque
telling me the story quietly
while we waited for doctors
to come collect from her body
signs of its rape: every morning
the poor shoe-
maker wakes
to find new shoes. And leaves.

I'd heard of copper beeches in books
and here am I living where they live.
It's again a start. I turn

corners, pages, leaving traces
with every step. I want the key.
Who knows this story?
Who is mindful of me?
I hurry when it starts to rain—
but, ok, it's stains you can read.

Coming Through, It Got Nice

There I stood. A corner, of course.
I thought trees' leaves went red and *then* Fall.
But here's wine-red and big in Spring,
And the red-gold sun *in* them, not on.
Above me in one, one sucked the sky
As if it were teeth, *its* teeth.
No wonder I was nervous standing there,
The whole world and me watching
Me not know ought to do anymore

While another one gnawed the hulls and husks
Of Fall just to make sure—so much
Squeaking and mouthing of the elements,
The sun spending itself in leafy wombs
And on the street, at that—

Oh bones, bones, fie
what to do w/ye now?

On the Way

I passed the yews at the funeral home,
a penile palisade bending this way and that
    (No, I've never seen that many laddies.
        Marry, a ladder! Let them all climb up!)
—it's a big wind this evening.

This afternoon I saw the man
I dreamed about nine years ago.
I trembled.
Rather than throw my phone number into his hat,
I chose not to be born
and went away.

Guitarcase, not hat.
Silent.

When I got here
where the only fencerow as far as I can see
catches the dark wind off the cornfields,
I hollered into it:
I WANT A SECOND CHANCE

Disbelief was in my voice.
I couldn't get rid of it.

May my life forgive me.
Joseph, sainted patron of travelers and of cuckolds,
may I like a nail in a carpenter's hand
go home.

Lecture

The invisibility
Of the movement
Is the guaranty
Of the mover's freedom
Here
In this world
Of appearances.

We have learned
About wind.
Let us turn
To candle flame
Which is also known
To waver.

Fire
Is the slave
Of the visible;
The visible
Is shackled by
Our eyes.

When at night
Your eyelids fall—
You must believe me—
The book beside
Your pillow sighs,

Visibly relieved.

In Some Respects Invisible, She Greets the Poet

I saw you last night at the Halloween party
And you didn't see me. That was me

Behind the clown white, me in my shoes. Unfortunately
You have to know a body first not to recognize her later.
Since I knew no one, it was a Trojan kind of triumph to pass unknown:
Great, the citadel's taken (second-story party)
But everybody's dragged shit-faced in the dust behind horses—
And here's Helen, moved to Iowa, eating candy corn.

She's blacked her body, blacked her head, the better to mourn
The loss of all except her stories. Wasn't it the Phaiakians' notion
That living is for giving poets something moving to sing? Horses asses
Or not (the shipping cost them dear), they freighted Odysseus
And his accumulated treasures back to patria and pater.
Some folks at home recognized him by his memories

And those who didn't died, suitable (heh) enemies.
Only each year's white face remembers all my me's.

Anyway, I saw you. In fact (or maybe figure) I walked smack into
Your face when I walked through the door. Ye gads! Earlier

I'd approached you, epistolary, at my desk where earlier
Still, laudatory, I'd approached you in your poems xeroxidary
And approach to redeem all approaching—you!

Here you are, too: I like the feel of the look of you in your blues,
Whether they're worn like last night with suspenders,
Or costumed lugubrious and squeamish on paper.

It's the feel of a picture in some book you make me remember,
Something I must have had as a kid—Huck Finn or Nigger Jim?
(Alright, sorry, a little goatish).
Darby O'Gill fiddling for shamrocks in a midnight quarry?
It occurred to me at 6 a.m. (I looked) you'd dressed up Amish.
Nevertheless, you looked a dandy. Me, I went home lonely

At 2 a.m. to write: I liked how you—and she—looked happy.

Trust

If I would be walking down the road
you told me to imagine and I would and find
a diner kind of teacup sitting on its saucer
in the middle then I would feel so good
in my life that is just like mine
I would walk right up and look into my face
eclipsing the sky in the tea in the cup
and say, "Thank you, I have enjoyed
imagining all this."

ii. Skin

The voice said, Cry. And he said, What shall I cry? All flesh is grass.

ISAIAH

The Uses of Things

When the stove clock hands sprawl
Wide with helpless want

The body is a wish.

When the light skins need along
The sink pipe's length

The body is a wish.

When the handles of the cupboard are
The parts of musn't touch

The body is a wish.

When the linoleum diagrams
The egg inside the egg

The body is the vehicle of a wish.

Terrible Two's

The sun dies and dies
Neither east nor west of anyplace.
It's there that I lie to you
With my whole body
(so you know I'm fervent).
Fever you understand, friend. I know.
That's why I've made my bed of that aromatic
Called feverfew. MANY ARE CALLED—no. Many
Were the animals on the ark,
Well used to their names by then.
I think I could use your body well, so
Full of its name—if I'd let me.
I'd come away with a name then, too, though
And death would look out through
My eyes. Dies and dies—I
Think it's worth it, A CHANCE WHICH DOES REDEEM—hey.
I think it'd be right nice
If you took off truth's clothes.
Then falsehood could flesh, teethe, force
The moon that rises
Flush at the sight of the moon that rises
In your fingernails, hum
"Over the river and through the flood,
To One People House we go."

Then little red truth-hood could say
NEITHER EAST NOR WEST OF ANYPLACE
THE SUN DIES AND DIES
And try to mean what she says.

Taking the Air

I almost died in a car crash here
Like Marc Bolan I used to love
Back when my father's vein crashed in
And his brain drowned in not enough air.

Since my wreck I haven't felt
Able to find myself.
Car 54, where are you?

Since way before my father's I've tried to drive
Fast off the edge
Of a not-flat self.

But a while before mine I found
I could sometimes stand to slow down
Sometimes get out in a strange small town
And walk through its evening air

To a house waiting
For me to find it
My toothbrush already waiting in it
My shoes at the foot of a me-shaped bed
And a curtained window
Slightly ajar.

Trojan Ho(u/r)se-keeping

On my red porch, a nickel.
Tails:
Tiny Monticello in the evening:
Geometries bear on a center
Where a secret sloughs itself a house.

Near the nickel, two yellow seeds.
Heads:
For these I find a hinged husk:
Not part of the mystery,
I don't take them in.

Inside, under lamplight,
I finger the nickel.
Monticello's windows are bare.
Where I live the windows are dark and give
Dark shapes of my body to me.
The gift gives: wanting to touch
Comes out of my body.

I live alone and
Someone was here.

> There was a comely note of poignancy in his insistence
> at the table that making love is like in its pleasure to
> the eating of an Orange.

It is the story that makes
The passing of time
Intelligible. So wait.

It is patently not
Enough to measure
The passing of time;

The glint of it
Will kill you.

The passing of time
Puts knives in the hands
That sweep (wait)

The watched face
Ticking off
Its tears.

Above a bowl of celadon,
Measured out in oranges eaten,
It's a sad time the mind slices
In order to tell it together again.

From the knife, pith.
From the knife, juice in its see-through placenta.
From the knife, oil to supple the skin.

Who will tell the story to keep
The lines between the stars in place,
The meanings from powdering down?

Who will ask: *What is the shape?*
Of the knives we find in our hands?

Orange-eater, the mind.
The mind would keep
The shape of this time
And lick its fingers after.

On Losing One's Life

My hand itches where the scab is coming off pink skin
and I am filling the room with heat and drinking, thin,
the first uncalculated drinks in years since when
in my other life where it was warm, I'd swallow
afternoons entire to evade their evenings; even so
such quickenings are only signs by which I know

that I am dead. For instance, when I read that the queen,
that Elizabeth of Roumania called Carmen Sylva
(given a Celtic brooch and a Balmoral shawl by Queen Victoria)
waved a napkin to a grazing cow she'd taken
for a loyal subject, then I knew. Quixote, aha, oho
I said; the life is more than windmills. I know

when one lives and when one's dead (as Lear
also de la Mancha, said). For me no feather
sirrah, nor mirror. Cordelia lives and I am dead;
these are clear.

Another House on Mother's Day

The clouds piled up on the top of the mountains
At the edge of the room I am living in,
The clouds piled up and didn't fall down.
Isn't this remarkable, and I have only just moved in.

Into the ground, into the bedroom ground
I pushed little seeds, round seeds and seeds of beets
Not round and not like anything except themselves.
This identity encourages me.

All around me, pink houses bud at the tips of the apple trees.
Lilacs bear their pyramidal hill towns above
A violet wood, a leaf-green village, its iris steeple.
A jay picks twigs

And I am the giant alone in her room.
Look, these tulips are my furniture
My furniture is eggs.

Look, my hands are the roof
My hair their roots
My knees the people

I make say: My heart's had many houses.
In this house, too, I room and mother me:
I have baked me a heart out of clay.

Forked Song

I am the one who is here.
I am eating the color of leaf.
Speared on a silver-tined fork I wave
a wheel of boiled carrot at the view—
at October and its mountain and its leaves.

The world fits me.
For my right ear is a notch,
a duplicated valley's V ascending askew,
earth opening like Venus' shell
bearing the bluegray of sea.

Hiss on shingle, it isn't. It is mountain there
blue in its distance, far and blue.
One heave of not-sea, one angle of un-wave.
Hush, you.

It turns itself to cloud, that sea
and sails, meet for my brow.
That is how I look when I think,
I think, and the several blues
fall right into my upturned eyes.

Maples in front of my nose
are for my nose, red and red.
The house behind me
suits the hair on my head.

For my left ear is an apple orchard,
a dozen trees in pairs escorting
a marble walk. The rock grows gray.
The red roundnesses make a slow music
as they fall down year after year,
a rhythm my heart knocks out untaught.

Shadows rise up and fall down with a swing, with a rock
like the sea's that roars on the palms of my hands
when I cup the world to my ears.
I wear the far field like a watch as I swallow
wheel after wheel of orange.
I am the one who is here.

Necessity With Respect to Yes

Posole soaks in a bowl and makes little kissing noises. This morning cats on the compost pile cried musically—at, to, for? Is a preposition appropriate here?

I am always so content in the mornings.

I lay listening before I awoke, shapes in air threading through ear, discerning whether not cats but babies of our kind cried, at which I should have to go out into the morning in bathrobe to be afraid at the world uncontained by the ideal, to find babies crying the waving strands of their singing on the compost pile.

Last night in the evening, in that high and uninhabited place of empty house and dark window, above the din of busyness, beneath the mountain with storm at its head, head-dress of cloud, purple and blue, a black-haired girl cried loudly over a low adobe wall into the evening—at, to, for? I came walking beneath her on the road below the wall and was stood before her crying out over the wall into the evening. Not at, not to, not for; neither to inquire nor to console, although these rose in the throat: only crying might go through air. She cried and cried. Only crying *could* go through air.

All the empty houses with doors ajar admitting wind and spilling darkness: inside the moment stillness and around it the crunching of foot on gravel, juniper and cedar threshing air; around it the balloon-like journey of child-voice upward into first dark. Far below and far behind it, noise of car-going and of dog.

A woman appeared and she walked into the yard of the house of the crying girl in silence and she put fist to door or to drawing of door on wall with no window: no sound. She caught there bringing fist to door, door to fist, wind blowing through the crying girl hair and dirt in the darkening wind, cloud and *could* drawn over all of our heads to the darker mountain, stayed.

The moment I rose to see cats a noise came from the kitchen. Posole soaking in a bowl fell over the edge in the kitchen where nobody was, in the white kitchen full of light. I lay back down as if told, not knowing.

Passing

It's winter and it will be for awhile.
A pheasant walks the edge of the little wood
In the company of sparrows.
She looks like the leaf-littered earth beneath the trees
Heard a voice it loved, woke up and walked.

(What are sparrows doing when they strop their beaks
On a branch like that?
Honing? Praying? Calling up spring?)

I was in the owl woods
Beneath the white pines. I found a skull with teeth
Like intricate meringues.

(The cat's white paw wraps richly around
Her sleeping and jowly white face.
Her blood shows pink through her ears.)

This skull bone grew in the right shape to live:
Casement for the cords of the coming spine
Arches like niches for what would be eyes—

This skull I hold
Grew full in love.

My quick bones know,
Cradled in their flesh
Curled in a yellow arm-chair
At a second-story window,

Fingers wrapped around the pen
That helps me grow the world up
Until, as now, it up and walks
Right through me.

Assumption

Was she lifted up? The rusty wheels humming their rubber
along the way she knew well—without her?
Was suddenly a shape (the very shape
her memories go on to make)
waiting for her where she'd tried to get (WITH CHILD A—)
knowing it was there that the world would begin?
The jig of her jaw, her hair like a hat, her
flat chest long thighs, high arch of each foot—
a perfect, waiting emptiness to comfort
her imperfection with its perfect fit—
was it waiting, the fruit
of putting on the usual boot,
of every day's eating an apple pared with a penknife,
mornings' left turn down the alley
occluded by an ark of a truck out of whose belly
come the parts of pizzas—is today
when the red bike became
the red seed swallowing its spokes, spinning the roots
of the possible, the centripetal
world?

iii. Mouth

An egg boiled very soft is not unwholesome.

JANE AUSTEN, *Emma*

I am no great Nebuchadnezzar, sir.
I have not much skill in grass.

SHAKESPEARE, *As You Like It*

Yew-berry

A mouth of round red flesh around it
The private green seed like a tongue inside it

The house holds the finger of its yew
Before its eye.

There's a shade for night
And a taken-away for the light of the day.

This is the lived in prayer.

Each morning, dutiful, the taken-away.
Every evening, blind.

The house mashes me to its mouth.
Between its fingers seed comes out.

Persephone Tells About
Some Going Downs

I took the subway downtown today.
My first time. I went down
not sure where to look, how to do.
      (I look, he's looking)
Mother with daughter, talking.
Change of station.
Mother with daughter laughing, walking.

I went to hear poets: kissing of cheeks.
Waving of books and fingers.
I didn't know a soul.
Paunchy bald men said
"I should apologize for this next poem, I'm
old-fashioned in my view of women," said
"Slut, oops, I should apologize, I

should say differently sexually abled, I
should say evil is done by the ethically challenged, I"
Ha-ha.
Everyone wants to be loved. Everyone wants to be included.
I want.
I look hopefully at faces
but everyone ha-ha's on cue.

My mother used to squeeze my sister's pimples
at the dinner table. Nobody screamed

out loud: we were supposed to enjoy
sausage, fried potatoes and each other.
Shame menu.
How doll parts on the sidewalk make me feel
sick, ha-ha.

When Alan Becker rang the doorbell and deposited me
on the New Year's Eve doorstep when I was sixteen
missing a shoe and a contact lens
sour puke and brittle leaves my raiment of glory
I couldn't stand up for my father to hit me.
My mother stood me up.
It wasn't anybody's first time, uh.

I don't know anybody in this city.
I don't know if I know how to know.
I just moved here. A room is home.
When they have nowhere else to go
roots—as in this narrow vase—go up.
      (I wish my hair (ha-ha) were grass)
I hope they reach some stone.

Now We Are Sick(x)

My hand is the tree
beneath the moon

in one hand a fork
in the other a spoon

My shoes are neat
beside my bed

ready to eat
wherever I'm fed

Sever this tree
from the root

bind my hand
hobble foot—

The moon will note the menu:
The girl was served

a male hors d'oeuvre
at a bedside venue

Present Company Occluded

He claims to hail from Ypsilanti.
I happen to know he thinks this a sexier way
to say Poughkeepsie, like being named Yvonne
with cigarettes and big breasts.
While he's talking, I realize I bought this plant
($7.77 at the local Star Market)
because it looks like my hair.
It isn't doing well.

Excuse me, I say, eventually.
I have to with a spoon
eat a jar of honey now,
I am that sad,
I am that far
from Planting Zone # 3.

The Au Pair Girl's Speech

Her secretary recorded it:
"Avocadro, alligator, palm;
for Monsieur Stevens, a squamous psalm."
Peeling Wallace with her tongue
The Lizard allows as how she knows a way
a shady way to say *alway*. "Sing,"
she said, "a concatenation of rind and bung;
transpose Limn Rime Spume Splay
into the tongue
of the flamingos
of the dingo-indigines
of the lip's ripe play."

iv. Nose

Gloucester: O let me kiss that hand!
Lear: Let me wipe it first; it smells of mortality.

SHAKESPEARE, *King Lear*

Point, Counterpoint

The staircase is a good place to cry.
You sit at the bottom
and all its dark climbing stands on your head,
its many indifferences
shoulders the better to cry on.

Touching street light lying in squares
on the stairs, you sob,
"I wanted to pick up light."
But you are myopic
and wanted to blow your nose.

Amen (On Christmas Day)

PROLOGUE

Rejoice all my hours—
let me, ok? (may I, mom)
I do, anyway—
a fair job.

THE PLAY

When in these them all mine *heures*
I do rejoice like smelling *fleurs*
well then bethink me mayhaps betide
of a redhaired man whom I much done sighed.

Last nighten kneed down before candle light;
cried for them I loves and have and lost,
glad of life the shining, shining on all that shineth not,
said, "It's ok god if you kill me now—I liked it a lot."

A man had toyed with me and I had broke inside
(if I'd a lyre the sing might song me together again);
I was the king's horse and by god as the king was a man
how he did flog me for so short a ride
     and breachéd sad.

So it's hey, nonny nonny—no, it is not. It's
the birth, the afterbirth, the maiden, the wench,
the blood on the sawdust, the warm stench.
I tried, you man, you imman, twice.
     Gimme flowers.

Miracle Whip, or Every Angel
His Own B(r)e(a)dspread

On the third day, I wrestled with the angel.
I wanted a fire by which to eat lunch.
Our lord of the fireplace, I called him,
giving *The New York Times* a nice crunch,
at which he sniffed, a quick intake of air
decreeing a piercing sound of smoke alarm
and the smell of burning hair.
Mine, of course. Look, I said,
I meant it as a compliment, a token
of my affection. He sucked a tooth, whereupon
the wire of the fire screen
impaled my ashy thumb. I mopped the blood.
He sipped his tea. He fanned a wing.
My eyes stung. Determinedly,
I put on my only pair of dress-up gloves
the better to wrench at a tiny lever
I took to be hooked to the flue.
More smoke alarm ensued.
The open door did not appease.
He flicked an ash from a feather
and one glove—nice black leather—
snagged on the ragged back of an andiron
and fell into the fire.
He wrinkled his nose and sneezed.

Too much is enough of him.
At this, the lamplight dimmed.
Hey, I only thought it, I said, no fair,

and gave him a friendly punch on the shoulder,
and sat in the rocker to examine my lunch.
Last night's fish with pickle and mayo,
some very soggy bread. He said,
Miracle of the loaves and fishes, anyone?
He who asks for bread won't get a stone
in his basket lunch instead?
(You should hear how he laughs:
Ha ha, exactly. And when he sneezed
it went *A choo,* matter of factly).
In the Bible, he said, you may recall
Jacob went some rounds with me. The gall—
"I will not let you go unless you bless me!"
Well, did you? I asked, my eye
on his undeniably beautiful hands,
remembering the particulars
of the Old Testament wrestling match.
"Somebody pressed his thumb into the sinew
of somebody's else's inner thigh,"
I tried. We both sort of sighed.

Later, after the labor of many hours
and the exercising of many powers,
we worked out who was who.
Bless the fire in the fire's place
that in the blessed does not subside.

Bud Cabal I

Hooray, it is Spring, it is beautiful here, hooray.
A note in my mailbox just wished me a blessed Beltane.
Next, I spied last night's length of dental floss.
Nexus? Abraxas, a tooth pow(d)er?
Incisor.[2] The alchemical hum of the power saw
eating its restorative breakfast below
(below, below, below, yo ho, yo ho—uh oh:
Dorothy, Kansas, wheat,
Demeter, Kore, dragon's teeth . . .).

Below. The guy next to me wearing *eau
de fume* on the subway. Toxic jacket (yellow
jackets busy around bags of pine bark out front;
the magnetic field of smell reducible to number.
Don't forget the = sign. Each piece
of former tree upended in the earth like teeth,
a necklace of the next thing,
and the magic winter coat of earth
weaves green ornament and worms stitch,
sometimes each other (like when 2=1,
when I=I in the night), and I walk down
the zipper stairs and those same numbers
request an erotic tune and I give it
to them *(you wear it so well),*
bloom in me anytime, bud)—
when he left, I breathed and closed the book

in which I'd written *"eau de fume,"*
stink not smoke. Chem-i-cal.

I want you to say that 'i' like 'ee'.
That is my blessing for you today.
Smile pretty. It is Spring morn
and you just with Abraxas
brushed your teeth.

Annunciation

I sat on a stone for too long. When I stood,
I smelled the smoke of cigar but saw
Only tombs and trees and squirrel-churned leaves.

An extra-long leaf of grass
pretended to metronome.
I wasn't fooled: I am learning to dance.

You may wonder: Why did I offer
to finger an angel's feathers?
His wings are terrible twin birds
perched on merely mortal shoulders.
It can't be easy.
It's the merely mortal that interests me
so I took a chance he'd lean and learn
the length of me. By the way,
he cared to dance.

A baby squeals. Its mother pets its father's leg.
Here, why shouldn't an angel smoke?
It's Sunday and he's free.

A cross could be four headstones in colloquy—
here, there is no need to beg:
one's necessity becomes another's.

Here, spiders web the carved-deep dates
and time the world with dew's prisms.
Refracted desire resurrects dead leaves.

There were no squirrels.
From here (between wings) you can tell (by the smoke)
all of the tombs are empty.

v. Ear

King Death has asses' ears.

THOMAS LOVELL BEDDOES

Invitation

Sparrows, plumbobs, as if lobbed fell
Out of the sky,

The nicety of past intimacy with arcs
Showing in their feathers.

The Lord hath shewn me a new heaven
and it has fallen into the old earth

Friend, the violets, something the sun coughed up,
Want you, *want* you.

Won't you go to them, now, this very evening?
It is the last of April

And the little water they keep green
In their secret place

Will avail the still birds nothing.

Shame

The sky made me aware of the throat of the sky,
The ribs of it the shape of an ocean's. The sigh,
The inhalation of the trees made me
Aware of the throat of the sky. I
Did not mean to lie.

In the bottom of the fat blue glass is the shape of
A peach pit, split, of a walnut shell halved, of
How I'd like my sex to appear where the
Blower broke his wand away from the
Aqua shape of glass.

I narrowed my eyes. I knew necessity
Had shaped me new today. I knew no one to
Whom I could say, "Come, I have finished
It, let us go." So, I simply sat, as I had
Before I'd begun my task.

The robin put its face in the grass, fast.
Through my hair I watch pigeons walk the green roof.
They gurgle the sky in their lavender throats.
Why should they get to, with no excuse?
When I think of glass

Birds I lose
The sky.

You Can Talk to the Animas

after Baudelaire's "Le Cygne"

The sky, yo ho, and the blue home of the noumena
Are yours tonight, my darling heart,
Monstrous echo of doughnut hole and evening's eternal mooting.
It begins, o my soul, with your buttocks when you sit
And with the soles of your feet when you stand.

The duck's wings drag the dust.
The duck's dry webs frotch, frotch against the pavement.
This is how to say parch, parch with the feet.
This is how to speak from the blue natal lake
In the too full heart to a sky both empty and blue.

To say something similar with something other, just remember
How your knee against the concrete left a dozen skin umbrellas,
Quivering pittances, peaks of flesh in a dozen desert valleys
In a sidewalk's terrain in a town you left behind
When you were six and ain't seen since.

The minute pebbles imbedded
In the knobs of your knees?
Incense offered the gods.

Dream of Hat and Mouth

A voice, maybe mine, is saying this:
"They are doing something else
But they are thinking about vi-o-lets."
"Vi-o-lets" means "vi-o-lence," I know.
Meanwhile, the brim of my young grandfather's hat
Exactly parallels his perfect arc of lip
An inch above it. No eyes, no nose
Only hat for a face and its edge's pendant echo smiled below.

He's standing watering posies with Mr. MacGregor's
Watering can. The fine strands of smiling
Water fall like hair. I can't see my little sister
But she is there—maybe in the feel of the water-hair
The finger's followed back to sprouting metal hat. Maybe
In the feel of the look of the nipple-eyed buds. Maybe
In the facts of the flowers themselves
That have to be, at last, what their witnesses are.

My sister is four. I'm six, myself.
We lie back to back in the single white bed
For punishment's afternoon nap. We whisper anyway.
White curtains frame the window's face,
A valance like my bangs on its brow. With a little switch of hair

I am turning the sun on and off.
She says I said so. I don't know.
It might have been the voice of the angry April day.

Apostrophe Antiphonal

Vessel vespine, vessel of wrath,
Ripe shrubs writhe here.

Here are stinging nettles
for after vespers singing.
Here on a virgal bed
evening parted. Herein
was surcease of pain.

Because versual,
because well-versed in verbs,
the world became a vestry
for vessels of wrath,
wraps of wasps and nettles
wreathing.

With these, vociferate view halloo.
In voragovorous voice,
with virginals twin
hymn Vesper vulpine,
in and out the volery
gleaming.

Rest on vetch, volatile voicer;
gladden bloomy heart:
wrath with wrath
writhe.

No voile, no vox celeste may
vocalize the night sky,
the volant and vulvulant,
the vulnerose, the
night sky, night sky.

Speaking (Out) of Feeling

I smile at my phone, for it has rung or rather, shrilled.
My heart fills as fondly I rehearse how I will tell
Whoever how like a creature lying brown
On my brown table is this receiver, my telephone.

It's Paddy the lockman, calling for Sears by night.
(My bad landlord, at last, repairs.) Paddy and I decide
The door's glass panes make a deadbolt dumb. He'll come
On Saturday and be home in time for the game.

This lock's been broken since mid-September.
Soon, Halloween. To get in I cut my finger
On the mouth my key cut in the screen.
To get out, there's only the mouth of the pumpkin—
For blade, a finger tongue of flame.

With the Tongues of Angels

He cut off my tongue and put it in my mouth
He said: Chew
I grew a spawn of bloody voices
when my stomach rumbled
I spoke with the tongues of his angels
the ones with wings like parrot tulips
their Italian faces just past Byzantine
in a puberty of angel growth

He painted all those angels and gilt their tongues
He painted for them lutes and cymbals
He said: Play her
I swallowed the raw sound of wing-whip
the severing sound of silk ripped
by feathers threshing air

I spewed a heaven hung with virgin
queens of heaven silent for the forced bloom
of sliced speech rooted as wing is fingered
deep into the shoulder blade occluding
larynx and labia equally. Tendrils between
the teeth eat each chawed symmetry.

Perspective won't do. All Italy and its
pistachioed flamingoed porticoed angelicoed among women blessed
won't to do express the angelic tumult

of spat tongues neatly paired and tapisseried winging duo
their way through now ringing air
the gigantic arc the now ringing reach
the vaulted great shape that is my mouth's first trying
the taste of my name.

In the beginning I laughed: Hee hee I yam
and I will be.

Covenant

The crow cawed when I came.
She whirled up
In the air like ash. I laughed
When I saw, too, what
Ear had heard
Like a promise been kept.

Think how you wear them, your ears.
Flesh in whorls.
Think what else
Beside her ocean
Of air a crow
Hears fulfilled.
Be glad. The earth
Is a fault in you
And wants to come forth in your name.

also by Liz Waldner

BOOKS

Saving the Appearances
Etym(bi)ology
Dark Would (the missing person)
Self and Simulacra
A Point Is That Which Has No Part
Homing Devices

CHAPBOOKS

Now How I Am an American
Representation
Read Only Memory
Call
With the Tongues of Angels
Memo (La)mento